THE *Carluccio's* COLLECTION

DESSERTS

ANTONIO & PRISCILLA CARLUCCIO

Dedicated to the memory of
photographer André Martin

Quadrille
PUBLISHING

Contents

All recipes are for 4 unless otherwise stated. Use either all metric or all imperial measures, as the two are not necessarily interchangeable.

Foreword

The Italian term for dessert is generally '*i dolci*' or '*il dolce*' – meaning 'sweet' – and these words can be found on almost all Italian menus. The tradition of having a pudding to finish the meal was adopted by the French in the last century because the Italians mainly like to finish their meal either with a sorbet, an ice-cream or usually with mixed fresh fruit in summer and baked pears or apples in the winter.

However, this does not mean that the Italians are short of dessert dishes and, although they do eat rich and more elaborate food they tend to eat thousands of these specialities during the day as a snack known as a '*capriccio*', or at the end of important celebratory dinners like weddings, communions, birthdays or namesday parties, or more traditionally during the religious festivities at Easter and Christmas.

Every region has traditional sweets that stem from local custom, the availability of local ingredients or the influences of neighbouring or related countries. Piedmont is very much influenced by France and boasts a large array of fine pâtisserie, like *bignole* – a tiny round choux pastry stuffed with zabaglione or cream and covered with sugar or other decorations. These are traditionally eaten on any grand occasion, but also during the day or in the numerous bars, where there is a big display of such delicacies.

Milan and Lombardy also have similar '*pasticceria alla crema*', with cream; or '*secca*', interesting dry biscuits based on nuts and even polenta. The traditional sweet of Milan is,

however, *panettone* – a cake baked for Christmas that is characteristically studded with candied orange peel, raisins and other candied fruits. It is extremely light and moist and should not be confused with fruit cake.

The entire area of the North East comprising the Veneto, Trentino and Alto Adige echoes the Austrian tradition – you may find there apple strudel and other specialities of Germanic origins. Liguria also has a *panettone* called '*genovese*' which looks much more like a fruit bread. In the Po Valley you may find *tiramisu* (meaning 'pick-me-up'), a mascarpone cheese-based dessert layered with sponge fingers dipped in strong coffee and liqueur.

Tuscany has a completely different approach, and its traditional sweet is the famous *panforte* (meaning 'strong bread'), a sticky cake that is flat like a torte and full of fruit, almonds and old-fashioned spices like cinnamon, cardamom, clove, nutmeg and even pepper. This is a remnant of the traditions of the Renaissance, when Tuscany imported Oriental spices. These spices were known only to the Tuscans, Ligurians and Venetians as a direct result of the marine Republics of Pisa, Genova and Venezia, all of which had strong trade links with the East. From Rome to the South, the Arabic and Greek influences are still visible today in their desserts.

The Southern marine Republic of Amalfi was responsible for the importing of spices and other products in a similar way to the northern republics in the areas of Campania and in the South in general, where the use of citrus fruits and nuts formed the base of the local sweets. Sicily, Calabria and Puglia were more under the strong influence of Arabic traditions.

Ice-cream was invented in Sicily as a direct result of sorbet – introduced by Arab princes who used the snow of Mount Etna blended with fruit syrups. The use of almonds and hazelnuts produced marzipan, plus milk products like ricotta and candied fruit were combined to form the famous *cassata* and *cannoli* in Sicily. All these regions (including Sardinia) have an array of biscuits and cakes based on wheat grain cooked with almonds and dried fruit which are baked for various occasions.

One could really say that the sweets and desserts of Italy are the witnesses of past cultures, left by invasions or trading and elaborated with the imagination and artisanal skill over the centuries using the local produce, primarily for nutritional reasons – but above all to make life happier!

My favourite dessert is still a simple piece of immaculately ripe fresh seasonal fruit. This way I can leave all the tempting sweets for the moments when I really feel the need to be spoiled. The famous *tiramisu* was certainly created by a mother watching her children in need of an uplifting element in their life. Try the following recipes – perhaps it will have the same effect on you!

Antonio Carluccio

Biscuits for ice-cream

Many Italian biscuits were almost purpose-built as foils for ice-cream. Here our saffron gelato is accompanied by outsize and eccentrically irregular savoiardi *(sponge fingers) studded with pine nuts. You could just as easily use* lingue di gatto *(cat's tongues) or any one of a number of thin* cialda *or wafers.*

Gelato allo Zafferano
SAFFRON ICE-CREAM

600 ml (1 pint) milk
pinch of saffron powder
8 egg yolks
125 g (4½ oz) caster sugar
175 ml (6 fl oz) double cream

Bring the milk to the boil in a pan and add the saffron. Beat the egg yolks and sugar together in a bowl until foamy and then gradually pour in the milk, stirring all the time, to obtain a velvety mixture.

Pour the mixture into a bowl set over a pan of very hot water, making sure the water is not touching the bowl, and cook, stirring, until it begins to thicken.

Add the cream, mix well, then transfer to an ice-cream maker and freeze. If you don't have an ice-cream maker, pour into a shallow bowl and place in the freezer for about 1 hour, until it is beginning to solidify around the edges. Whisk it well with a fork, then return to the freezer. Repeat this process 3 times and then freeze until firm.
Serves 6

This is more my own contribution to the ice-cream world more than a traditional speciality. It was my aim to celebrate saffron, one of the world's most sought after and expensive spices.

Saffron

Saffron has enjoyed a reputation as the king of spices since Egyptian times and was used as currency by the Doges of Venice. Its high price is due to the fact that it has to be picked by hand and that it takes the stigmas of half a million Crocus sativus (which only flowers for two weeks) to make a kilo. Once picked, the stigmas are dried over a low heat, and this reduces their overall weight by 80 per cent.

The saffron stigmas are sold in small packets of 1 gram in weight or reduced to a powder. It is best to get strands as they give the best flavour and colour. Soak them in water to release the colour and taste before adding them to the dish with the liquid.

Possibly the most famous Italian recipe using saffron is the Milanese risotto allo zafferano. It is also used in fish sauces and soups, which are really lifted by the warm colour and aroma imparted by the spice.

Most saffron is grown in La Mancha in Spain, but Italian saffron comes from the Abruzzi region, and more recently Sardinia, where the longest, richest-coloured stigmas of outstanding quality can be found.

Zabaglione Gelato
ZABAGLIONE ICE-CREAM

16–18 free-range egg yolks
300 g (10½ oz) caster sugar
200 ml (7 fl oz) Moscato Passito di Pantelleria or Marsala
500 ml (18 fl oz) whipping cream

Put the egg yolks and sugar in a large bowl and whisk with a hand-held electric beater or a whisk until foamy and doubled in volume. Put the bowl over a saucepan of gently simmering water, making sure the water does not touch the base of the bowl. Continue to whisk until the mixture is very thick and has a homogeneous, creamy but not crumbly texture. It is crucial not to let it overheat or you will end up with scrambled eggs.

Leave to cool, then fold in the Moscato Passito di Pantelleria or Marsala. Whip the cream until it forms soft peaks and then fold it into the mixture.

Place in an ice-cream maker and freeze. If you do not have an ice-cream maker, transfer the mixture to a shallow bowl and place in the freezer for about 1 hour, until it is beginning to solidify around the edges. Whisk it well with a fork, then remove from the freezer. Repeat this process 3 times and then freeze until firm.

Serves 6-8

Eggs

Eggs are valued for their versatility in the Italian kitchen as they can be boiled, baked, scrambled, fried and poached, made into omelettes as well as being used in cakes, pasta, custards, ice-cream and mayonnaise, scrambled in soups or even used to thicken sauces.

Perhaps the most remarkable dish they are used for is this zabaglione, where the yolks are beaten in a bain-marie with sugar and marsala, sherry or Moscato to make one of the most desirable desserts.

Italians use eggs a lot but, curiously, seldom at breakfast. At Easter-time, eggs feature prominently as symbols of new life.

Eggs are a complete food and this recipe in their honour is always a success.

Tiramisu
COFFEE AND CREAM DESSERT

3 egg yolks
100 g (3½ oz) caster sugar
1 tsp vanilla sugar or a few drops of vanilla extract
100 ml (3½ fl oz) single cream
500 g (1 lb) mascarpone cheese
6 cups of cold strong espresso coffee
4 tbsp coffee liqueur, such as kahlúa
20 savoiardi biscuits
cocoa powder for dusting

Beat the egg yolks with the caster sugar and vanilla sugar until thick and mousse-like. Beat the single cream into the mascarpone to loosen it, then carefully fold in the egg yolk mixture.

Spread half the mixture over the base of a large shallow serving dish. Mix the espresso coffee and liqueur together in a shallow dish and briefly dip in the savoiardi biscuits one by one, putting them immediately on top of the layer of mascarpone.

When you have used up all the biscuits, spread the rest of the mascarpone mixture on top to cover them completely and then chill.

Before serving, dust the tiramisu generously with cocoa powder. You could make individual portions in glasses, cups or other small containers.

Serves 6

Mascarpone

Initially only made in southern Lombardy, in the province of Lodi, mascarpone cheese is now produced in various Italian regions. Made within 24 hours of milking from pasteurized cream coagulated with citric or 5 per cent tartaric acid, it is a very soft cheese which once it is made has to be consumed immediately. One hundred litres (22 gallons) of cream produce 40-50 kg (90-110 lb) of mascarpone with a fat content of 50 per cent and above. Mascarpone is seldom used as cheese, but is extremely valuable as an ingredient for sweets and desserts, one of the most famous being this tiramisu. It is also used, together with herbs, as a filling for ravioli or as a thickener for sauces. In the past it was packed in small fabric containers, but it is now sold in jars or plastic containers.

Budino di Rosa

ROSA'S PUDDING

1 litre (1¾ pints) milk

300 g (10½ oz) sugar

100 g (3½ oz) 00 (doppio zero) flour

100 g (3½ oz) powdered bitter chocolate

grated zest of 1 lemon

yolks of 3 eggs

5 tbsp Amaretto liqueur

16 savoiardi biscuits

Amaretto

This is the most typical of Italian liqueurs taken, mostly by ladies, as a digestif after a meal. Like the biscuits of the same name, it is based on bitter almonds, but the liqueur also contains other added fruit essences and aromatic herbs. With its very distinctive bitter almond taste, it is also often added to desserts, fruit salads, puddings and cocktails.

Put the milk and 100 g (3½ oz) of the sugar in a pan, then stir in the flour and chocolate. Stir until smooth and bring to the boil, stirring continuously. Off the heat, stir in the lemon zest and egg yolks and mix well.

In a small bowl, mix the liqueur with an equal amount of water. Dip the biscuits briefly in this mixture and use them to line a pudding mould. Pour the milk mixture into the lined mould and chill to set.

When firmly set, about 2-3 hours, turn it over and remove it from the mould (dipping it first very briefly in hot water will help).

Dissolve the remaining sugar in 4 tablespoons of water and cook until it begins to brown to a caramel. Pour this over the pudding and leave to set before serving.

Serves 6

This is a pudding from Rosa, the pasta queen of the Ristorante Ardenga in Diolo, Emilia-Romagna. It is simple but highly effective.

Panna Cotta

BAKED CREAM

1 leaf of gelatine
500 ml (18 fl oz) single cream
45 g (1½ oz) sugar
1 vanilla pod
1 tsp vanilla essence
1 tbsp dark rum
strips of candied orange peel or fresh berries to decorate

Soak the gelatine leaf in a little cold water until soft.

In a heavy-based pan, mix the cream with the sugar and vanilla pod and essence. Bring to the boil. Take off the heat and add the soaked gelatine leaf and the rum. Stir well until the gelatine has dissolved. Pass through a fine sieve and pour into 4-6 dariole moulds. Put in the refrigerator to set.

To serve, decorate with small pieces of candied orange peel or, if you prefer, with fresh berries.

Serves 4-6

This is currently one of the most fashionable of Italian desserts both in Italy and abroad, possibly because it is so easy to make as well as good to eat.

Fichi al Forno

BAKED FIGS

12 ripe but firm, large fresh figs, peeled
300 g (10½ oz) caster sugar
zest and juice of 1 lemon
mascarpone cheese or lightly whipped double cream, to serve (optional)

Preheat the oven to 250°C/475°F/gas9. Put the figs closely together on a small baking tray and cover them evenly with the sugar. Sprinkle the lemon juice over them and half the lemon zest, cut into thin strips. Finely dice the remaining lemon zest and set aside. Bake the figs for 20 minutes, until the sugar is foaming.

Remove from the oven, spoon a little of the caramelized sugar on to each fig and sprinkle over the remaining lemon zest. Put back in the oven for another 5 minutes.

Remove and transfer to a nice porcelain plate, pour the cooking juices over and leave to cool, then refrigerate. Serve with a dollop of mascarpone or lightly whipped double cream, if desired.

This great classic dessert is made with very simple ingredients indeed. However, the figs have to be impeccably ripe and of good quality.

Fig

The finest figs are those eaten ripe from the plant, a rarity these days as so much fruit is picked unripe for long transportation. Originally from Syria, the fig was spread all over the world by the Romans and it is now grown in Italy in the regions of Puglia, Calabria and Sicily.

Fresh figs are very popular eaten simply as a fruit, with Parma ham and in fruit salads and tarts. My favourite recipe for dried figs is baked in the oven until brown in colour, then cut in half and served with almonds. Figs soaked in a syrup of orange juice and honey and then boiled for about 5 minutes are also delicious.

Melecotogne in Composta

QUINCE COMPOTE

Quince

In the past, the quince was much used in the kitchen, especially to make sauces for roasted meats. Today, although it is still cultivated and is available on the market stalls of Italy in the autumn, it no longer holds the culinary position it once enjoyed. The small trees, with their regularly shaped leaves, bear pear- and apple-shaped fruit (hence the names mela *or* pera*), with downy yellow skin that rubs down to a shine. It has a wonderful scent, although its flesh is too sour to eat raw and once cut it discolours rapidly, so a few drops of lemon juice need to be sprinkled over it.*

1 kg (2¼ lb) quinces, quartered, peeled and deseeded
400 g (14 oz) caster sugar
1 lemon, preferably organically grown
1 cinnamon stick (optional)
double cream, mascarpone cheese or plain yoghurt, to serve

Put the quinces in a large pan and add enough water to reach a third of the way up the fruit. Add the sugar and squeeze in the juice from the lemon, then add the squeezed-out lemon halves and the cinnamon stick, if using. Bring to the boil, cover and simmer for about 15 minutes, until the quinces are soft but still hold their shape. Check by inserting a knife from time to time. Remove the lemon halves and leave to cool.

Serve chilled with some double cream or mascarpone or even with plain yoghurt.

Serves 10

The quince never ripens to a satisfactory point and so needs a great deal of sugar to preserve it. For this reason it is best enjoyed as a jam, compote or fruit butter or paste – *cotognata*, wonderful as an accompaniment to cheese.

Marroni al Mascarpone
CANDIED CHESTNUTS WITH MASCARPONE

2 egg yolks

100 g (3½ oz) caster sugar

1 tsp vanilla sugar

2 tbsp whisky

4 tbsp single cream

400 g (14 oz) mascarpone cheese

12 whole chestnuts in syrup or marrons glacés

12 fresh bay leaves

Beat the egg yolks with the caster sugar, vanilla sugar and whisky to obtain a smooth cream. Beat the single cream into the mascarpone to soften it and then carefully fold in the egg yolk mixture. Put the mixture into a piping bag and pipe 3 equal dollops on to each dessert plate. Top with the chestnuts and then decorate with the bay leaves.

This is a dessert with abundant calories, to be served mainly in winter after a very light meal. The whisky flavouring is very much my own idea, grappa would be more traditional.

Chestnut

No walk in the mountains during the months of October and November is complete without collecting a few pounds of chestnuts. This nut grows on huge trees that are also valued for their precious wood by the furniture industry. The sweet chestnut tree is common in the Apennines and Pre-Alps and when the nuts are in season they are either roasted or boiled and consumed in huge quantities.

As well as the common chestnut, there is another variety called marroni *which is much used in the kitchen. Marroni have a spiky shell and grow singly, whereas ordinary chestnuts grow in clusters. They are used to make* marroni canditi *(marrons glacés or candied chestnuts), which are very popular at Christmas time. Marroni canditi are very expensive because in the process of making them many get broken and only the whole ones are eventually sold.*

Parmigiano con le Pere e Noci

PARMESAN CHEESE WITH PEARS AND WALNUTS

Parmigiano Reggiano

Parmigiano reggiano used to be made only between 1 April and 11 November, but today it can be produced throughout the year. However, the cows that produce the milk for parmigiano reggiano can only be fed on grass and hay, and parmigiano reggiano does not contain any additives to aid fermentation.

Parmesan is not only grated over most Italian pasta dishes, except fish ones, but it is also used to flavour omelettes, grated and added to other ingredients as a filling, cut or shaved into slices and sprinkled on carpaccios and into salads. It is also delicious eaten with fruit such as pears, grapes, figs, walnuts or hazelnuts, or even dressed with a few drops of balsamic vinegar.

200 g (7 oz) parmesan cheese
4 ripe Williams pears
100 g (3½ oz) fresh walnuts, peeled
good *pane di campagna* (country bread), to serve

Break the parmesan cheese into splinters. Peel the pears, then core and slice them.

Assemble the cheese, pears and walnuts on each plate and serve with good country bread.

This combination is ideal for when new-season walnuts are available and are fresh enough to peel. The skin should come off easily in your fingers. Not really a recipe, this is just an idea for a dessert and one that is popular in Emilia-Romagna, where the cheese comes from.

Piles of parmigiano reggiano cheeses stacked in the large airy maturing rooms, called 'cathedrals'. For the first 6–7 months there each cheese is turned every 4–5 days and after that every 10–12 days.

Pasta di Mandorle

MARZIPAN

1 kg (2¼ lb) fresh shelled sweet almonds
400 g (14 oz) icing sugar
½ tsp vanilla extract
cornflour for dusting

Put the almonds in a large pan of boiling water and simmer for 5 minutes. Drain and leave to cool, then peel them. The skins should come off easily.

In a food processor, grind the nuts to a slightly coarse mixture. Stir in the icing sugar and vanilla extract, then turn out on a work surface and knead to a dough, dusting with cornflour to prevent sticking.

At this stage you can roll out the almond paste and make it into shapes, dusting your hands and the work surface with icing sugar to prevent sticking, sandwich it around chopped citron peel as here, say, or you can store it in an airtight container in the fridge until required. Should you want to colour the marzipan, use good non-synthetic food colouring. Makes about 1.25 kg (2¾ lb)

Use fresh almonds and grind them yourself rather than buy ready-ground, which dry out quickly.

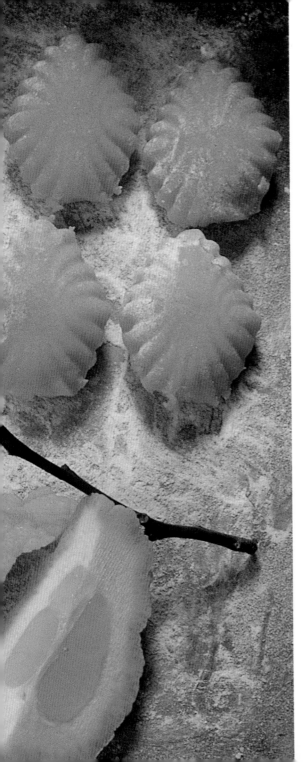

Orzata

ALMOND MILK DRINK

165 g (5½ oz) sweet almond paste
600 ml (1 pint) water

Put the almond paste and water in a liquidizer and blend until it forms a white, milky fluid. If it is too strong, dilute with a little more water.

This wonderfully refreshing summer drink was originally made with barley, but now a thick, sugared almond paste is more likely to be used. It is also called *latte di mandorle*, or almond milk.

Baba Vesuvio

RUM BABA

Yeast

There are two types of yeast, one natural and one synthetic. They both have the task, through their fermentation, of producing bubbles in the combination of flour and water, or other ingredients, in order to raise and aerate the mixture and thus obtain a softness in the baked goods. Bread without yeast would be flat and hard and inedible. The best yeast is a by-product of making beer. The pinky-brown substance is diluted with water and mixed with whatever is to be baked. It is important to allow the fermentation to take place in a warm place, before putting the dough in a hot oven. Synthetic yeast does not need such pre-fermentation.

25 g (¾ oz) fresh brewers' yeast (or the equivalent of dried)

100 ml (3½ fl oz) lukewarm milk

300 g (10½ oz) 00 (doppio zero) flour, plus more for dusting

pinch of salt

85 g (3 oz) sugar

100 g (3½ oz) melted butter, plus more for greasing

1 tbsp grated lemon zest

5 eggs

5 tbsp warmed apricot jelly

FOR THE SYRUP:

250 g (9 oz) caster sugar

grated zest of 1 orange

300 ml (½ pint) dark rum

Dissolve the yeast in the lukewarm milk and gradually add to the flour, salt and sugar in a large bowl. Mix thoroughly. Add the butter and lemon zest. Mix well. Gradually add the eggs, one by one, and work well to obtain a smooth dough. Leave covered with a cloth in a warm place until doubled in size, about 2 hours.

Punch the risen dough and work with your hands to knock out the air built up during rising. Grease a suitably shaped ovenproof mould with butter and then dust it with flour. Put the dough into it (it should only fill it about three-quarters full). Leave to rise again, until the dough reaches the top of the mould. Preheat the oven to 200°C/400°F/gas6 and bake the baba for 40 minutes.

While the baba is baking, make the syrup: put the sugar in a pan with 600 ml (1 pint) water and the orange zest. Bring to the boil, then

remove from the heat and stir in the rum.

Remove the baba from the oven and, while it is still warm, pour half of the syrup over it. Leave for a few minutes to let the baba absorb the syrup, then pour the remaining syrup over it. Place the baba on a serving dish and brush with the apricot jelly. Chill briefly and serve. It should have a springy texture.

Serves 10-12

Struffoli Napoletani

NEAPOLITAN FRIED PASTRIES

5 eggs

3 tbsp granulated sugar

500 g (1 lb 1½ oz) flour

grated zest of 1 lemon and 1 orange

pinch of salt

1 tbsp pure alcohol (if not available, strong vodka will do)

oil for deep-frying

50 g (2 oz) cedro (candied citron peel)

25 g (¾ oz) little edible silver balls, to decorate

FOR THE CARAMEL:

100 g (3½ oz) sugar

250 g (9 oz) honey

In a large bowl, beat the eggs with the sugar, then gradually mix in the flour to make a smooth dough. Add the citrus zest, the salt and the alcohol. Knead well for 3 or 4 minutes and roll into a ball. Cover and leave to rest for 2 hours in a cool place.

Roll the dough with your hand into sausages shapes about 1 cm (½ inch) in diameter. Cut into pieces about 1 cm (½ inch) long.

In a small pan, pour in oil to a depth of 2-3 cm (¾ – 1¼ inches) and heat until moderately hot. Deep-fry the pieces of dough in batches until lightly browned. Remove and drain on absorbent paper.

To make the caramel: in a large heavy-based pan, heat the sugar and honey with 2 tablespoons of water until the liquid becomes clear. Add the struffoli and the chopped peel. Stir carefully until all the struffoli are coated with caramel. Arrange in the form of a crown on a serving plate, decorate with silver balls (not too many) and leave to cool.

Citron

The candied peel of the cedro or citron is used in the famous Italian cakes panettone and panforte, in Cassata and Cannoli (see the recipes on pages 38 and 41), as well as in a filling for tarts mixed with ricotta, and to make a drink called cedrata. The flowers of the citron plant produce an essence used to flavour confectionery and in the making of perfumes.

Ravioli Fritti Sardi con Miele

FRIED SARDINIAN PECORINO RAVIOLI WITH HONEY

Honey

*Castagno or chestnut honey is a very dark
and heavily scented honey with a slightly
bitter flavour, which is made all over Italy
when the chestnut tree is in bloom.
Piedmont, with its hilly terrain, produces a
lot of good-quality chestnut honey.
Honey is easily digestible and includes
many nutritionally valuable trace elements
and proteins. It is mostly used in the
preparation of biscuits and creams, and to
sweeten drinks. I add it to sauerkraut and
spread it on roast pork to caramelize the
skin. It is, however, at its most delicious in
the Neapolitan speciality Struffoli (see the
recipe on page 35).*

200 g (7 oz) pecorino cheese, thinly sliced
olive oil for frying
chestnut honey or other honey, to serve
FOR THE PASTRY:
300 g (10½ oz) flour, preferably type 00 (doppio zero)
3 eggs
100 g (3½ oz) caster sugar

First make the pastry: sift the flour, make a well in the centre and add
the eggs and sugar. Gradually draw in the flour to make a smooth
dough, similar to pasta dough. Roll it out to 3 mm (⅛ inch) thick and
cut out 16 circles about 12.5 cm (5 inches) in diameter.

Divide the pecorino cheese between half the pastry circles. Brush
the edges of the pastry with water and cover with the remaining pieces
of pastry, pressing down gently around the edges to seal.

Heat a generous quantity of olive oil in a large frying pan and fry the
pastries until golden brown on both sides. Serve hot with honey.
Makes 8

These little pastries filled with pecorino cheese
are a Sardinian speciality, served with honey.
They are delicious after a light meal.

Cassata

SICILIAN CASSATA

icing sugar for dusting

250 g (9 oz) marzipan

1 round of sponge cake, about 20 cm (8 inches) in
    diameter and 5 mm (¼ inch) thick

2 tbsp Marsala

375 g (13 oz) ricotta cheese

100 g (3½ oz) caster sugar

½ tsp vanilla extract

25 g (¾ oz) candied orange peel, chopped

25 g (¾ oz) candied citron peel, chopped

25 g (¾ oz) plain chocolate, chopped

angelica and extra candied peel, to decorate

FOR THE ICING:

125 g (4½ oz) icing sugar

1 egg white

1 tsp lemon juice

15 g (½ oz) plain flour

Dust with icing sugar a 20 cm (8 inch) diameter pie
dish with sloping sides. Divide the marzipan in two
and knead one half to a smooth dough, then roll
this out until it is 5 mm (½ inch) thick. Use it to line
the sides of the dish, cutting it to fit.

Take the sponge cake round and place it on the
bottom of the dish, trimming it around the edges if
necessary to make it fit. Sprinkle the Marsala over
the cake.

Put the ricotta in a bowl and crush it with a fork. Add the caster sugar and vanilla extract and mix until it becomes slightly moist and binds together well. Pass the mixture through a sieve, then stir in the candied peel and chocolate. Spoon the ricotta mixture over the sponge in the dish.

Knead the remaining marzipan, roll it out and use to cover the filling. Turn the cassata upside down on to a serving plate so that the sponge that was at the bottom is now at the top.

To make the icing, sift the icing sugar into a bowl and mix in the egg white and lemon juice. Add the flour gradually to thicken it slightly. Mix well.

Immediately pour the icing mixture over the cassata to cover the top and sides. Decorate with candied peel and angelica, then leave for a couple of hours for the icing to set.

There are two versions of cassata, both of which originate from Sicily. One is this cake made with marzipan, ricotta and candied fruit, while the other is a much later development made with ice-cream.

Cannoli

SICILIAN CANNOLI

15 g (½ oz) lard or butter

1 tbsp sugar

3 tbsp dry white wine

1 tsp white wine vinegar

150 g (5 oz) type 00 (doppio zero) flour

1 tbsp cocoa powder

1 egg, beaten

vegetable oil for deep-frying

FOR THE FILLING:

600 g (1 lb 5 oz) ricotta cheese, sieved

300 g (10½ oz) caster sugar

55 g (1¾ oz) candied citrus peel, chopped

55 g (1¾ oz) dark chocolate, chopped into small pieces

Cannoli

*Cannoli is probably the best-known Sicilian dessert and gets its name from the fact that it is deep-fried around a piece of cane (*canna*). It used only to be made for* Carnevale *(carnival) and for the feast day of San Carlo. Now it is eaten all year round, not only after meals, but also as a snack.*

Cream together the lard or butter and sugar until light, then mix in the wine and vinegar. Fold in the flour and cocoa and knead to form a dough. Cover with cling film and rest in the refrigerator for 30 minutes.

Roll out the dough into a large sheet about 2 mm (½ inch) thick and cut into 15 rectangles about 10 x 6 cm (4 x 2½ inches). Wrap each piece of pastry around a length of cane, sealing the join with beaten egg.

Heat the oil in a large deep pan, making sure there is enough to cover the cannoli. When the oil is very hot, add the cannoli, a few at a time, and deep-fry until crisp and golden brown – 1½ –2 minutes. Drain on paper towels and leave to cool. Remove the canes.

To make the filling: with a fork, mix the sugar, peel and chocolate into the cheese. Fill cannoli with the mixture. Serve cool but not chilled. Makes 15

Confettura di Lamponi

RASPBERRY JAM

Sottobosco

This is a fairly recent Italian term used to describe all the wild soft fruit one may find in the woods, such as wild strawberries, wild raspberries, wild blackberries, etc. It is also applied to a salad made of such fruit, or sauces incorporating the fruit for use in and with cakes and tarts. The term has even found use in the language of wine-tasting, to evoke flavours reminiscent of woodland like moss and fungus.

700 g (1 ½ lb) raspberries, preferably wild

700 g (1 ½ lb) caster sugar

Put the fruit and sugar in a heavy-based pan over a low heat and stir with a wooden spoon to break up the fruit. Increase the heat slightly and, when it begins to boil, skim off the foam from the surface. Simmer for about 30 minutes, then check the setting point by putting a teaspoonful on a small plate: if it solidifies when cool, it is ready.

Put into sterilized jars and cover with waxed paper discs. Leave until completely cold and then seal.

Makes 1 kg (2lb 3oz)

This is probably the most delightful of jams for taste and colour. In the mountainous regions of northern Italy it is still possible to pick your own wild raspberries and they have a remarkably intense flavour, particularly good in this jam. You may also be able to buy them in a market, which will certainly be easier although they will not taste as good.

Confettura di Castagne
CHESTNUT JAM

1.25 kg (2½ lb) fresh chestnuts
a few bay leaves
1.25 kg (2½ lb) caster sugar
1 vanilla pod, slit open lengthwise

Slit the skins of the chestnuts, boil for 5 minutes and peel while still hot, removing both outer and thin inner skin. Cook the chestnuts with the bay leaves in lightly salted boiling water for 30 minutes. Drain and leave to cool. Remove any remaining pieces of skin with the tip of a knife. Pass the chestnuts through a sieve to obtain a fairly dry purée.

Put sugar and vanilla pod in a heavy pan with 200 ml (7 fl oz) water. Stir over moderate heat until a pale, translucent syrup. Discard vanilla and add the chestnut purée. Cook gently, stirring often, for 30 minutes.

Pour the jam into sterilized jars and cover with waxed paper discs. Leave until completely cold and then seal.
Makes 2 kg (2 lb 3 oz)

My granny used to make this jam and we children would eat it on its own by the spoonful as a treat. It was also even sometimes served with double cream as a pretty calorific dessert.

Vanilla

If you cannot get hold of vanilla pods, then look for good quality vanilla essence, which is very expensive and strong and should be used with care. There is also a powdered version for dishes where the seeds and colour of the vanilla are not wanted. Synthetic versions of vanilla essence and powder are far weaker than the real thing.

Vanilla is used almost exclusively in the making of sweets, chocolate, creams, ice-creams, custards and patisserie. It is also possible to use the pods to flavour sugar by placing one or two pods in an airtight jar until the sugar has absorbed the scent.

This vanilla sugar can then be used for making custards, or for panna cotta (see page 16), or added to all sorts of puddings and cakes.

Confettura di Pere Cotogne

PIEDMONTESE MIXED FRUIT JAM

2 litres (3½ pints) fresh red grape juice
1 kg (2¼ lb) quinces, peeled, cored and chopped
1 kg (2¼ lb) ripe plums, stoned and chopped
500 g (1 lb) pears, peeled, cored and chopped
1 cinnamon stick
finely grated zest of 2 lemons
200 g (7 oz) walnut halves
2 kg (2¼ lb) caster sugar

Put the grape juice, fruit, cinnamon stick, lemon zest and walnuts into a large pan, preferably a copper preserving pan. Cook slowly for 1 hour, then add the sugar and cook over a gentle heat for a few hours, stirring often to prevent sticking, until the mixture is very thick and almost brown in colour and all the fruit has dissolved.

Put in sterilized jars and cover with waxed paper discs. Leave until completely cold, then seal.

Makes about 5 kg (11 lb)

Copper pans hanging in the kitchen of a friend of ours in Naples.

Plums, Prunes

As well as being eaten fresh on their own, plums can be baked in sweets or simply stewed with sugar or made into jam. The dried version of the fruit, the prune, is used in confectionery and for baking. They are wonderful preserved in brandy, when they can be eaten with ice-cream or with creamy desserts, or simply soaked in water as an accompaniment to pork or game dishes. They are also used to make slivovitz, a well-known Yugoslavian type of schnapps.

This was made in the autumn during the grape harvest so freshly pressed grape juice and other autumnal fruits could be used.

Frutta Sciroppata
FRUITS IN SYRUP

1 kg (2¼ lb) ripe fruit, such as peaches, plums and kumquats
800 g (1¾ lb) caster sugar
1 vanilla pod

If using peaches, blanch them briefly in boiling water, then skin and halve them and remove the stone.

Put the sugar and vanilla pod in a large pan with 1 litre (1¾ pints) of water and heat gently until the sugar has completely dissolved. Add the fruit and cook gently until just tender – anything from 25 minutes for the softest fruit to 40 minutes for harder ones. Remove the fruit with a slotted spoon and set aside. Increase the heat and boil the liquid until reduced in volume by a third. Reduce the heat again, put the fruit back in the pan and cook over a very low heat for another 30 minutes.

Transfer to a sterilized jar, seal and store in a cool place until needed. Serve with ice-cream or Panna Cotta (page 16).
Makes enough to fill a 1.5 kg (3lb 5oz) jar

This is half way between a compote and crystallized fruit. The secret is to achieve a degree of sugar concentration in the liquid so that it functions as a preservative. The fruit should keep its shape.

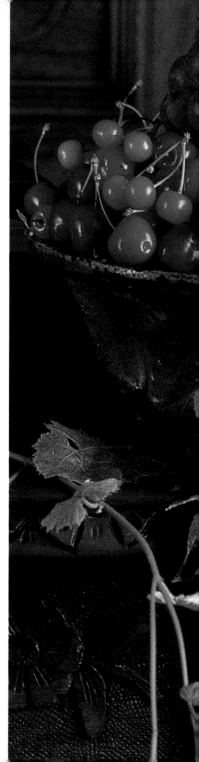

Peach, Nectarine

*Peaches and nectarines are mostly eaten on
their own or in fruit salads, but peaches are
more widely used in the kitchen than
nectarines. In Piedmont peaches are sliced,
dipped in red wine and sprinkled with a
little sugar before being eaten. They can
also be halved, stuffed with a mixture of
beaten egg, crumbled amaretti, cocoa
powder and sugar, then baked in the oven.
Peaches are pulped to make* succo di pesca,
*which is mixed with champagne to make
the famous Bellini cocktail. Peaches are
also used to make jam and a solid paste
called* pasta di frutta, *as well as being dried
for long keeping.*

Frutta sotto Spirito

FRUIT IN ALCOHOL

It is best to use very high spirit (95 per cent alcohol) for this, which is readily available in Italy but not everywhere. You should always use ripe fruit no larger than a small tangerine. Grapes, cherries, apricots, and dried fruits such as raisins are ideal. Soft fruits such as berries are not suitable.

Pack the fruit tightly into a sterilized preserving jar, then pour over the alcohol and seal the jar. The rest is done by time, and 3 months is the minimum it should be left.

Serve the fruit in small glasses either on its own or accompanied by thick cream or ice-cream. It should not be given to children; this is a serious grown-up affair!

Left to right: apricots, cherries and grapes in alcohol.

Glossary of Dessert Ingredients

***Albicocca, Armelline** / Apricot, Apricot Kernel*
Apricots were brought to Italy from China by the Arabs. It is a fruit with many varieties, including Cafona and Reale d'Imola. It ripens over the three months between June and September, depending on the variety. The velvety orangey-yellow-skinned and large-stoned fruit has a juiciness and flavour rivalled only by the peach. Italy produces about 200,000 tonnes of apricots every year, making it one of the largest producers in the world. It is grown in the warm sunny regions of Campania and Emilia-Romagna, two of the most fertile regions of Italy, as well as in Piedmont, Basilicata and Sicily.

***Amarena, Marasca, Visciola, Ciliegia Acida** / Morello Cherry, Maraschino Cherry, Montmorency Cherry, Sour Cherry*
Even when ripe, the morello cherry still tastes sour, although it leaves a wonderful flavour in the mouth. It is this very bitterness that makes these cherries ideal for preserving and for making syrups and jams that are used in the making of pastries, drinks and ice-cream. The famous Maraschino liqueur is made with a variety of the sour cherry called Marasca. The best variety is the Montmorency, which is cultivated in the hilly regions of Italy and exported to Germany where it is used to make the liqueur Kirsch.

***Arancia** / Orange*
Oranges have a relatively short history in the Mediterranean and it was only in the last century or two that the culture of oranges began in Sicily and Campania – now two of the main areas of production in Italy. For successful cultivation oranges need sub-tropical temperatures, and well-drained and rich organic soil with a modern system of irrigation.

The orange is an extremely versatile fruit which can be eaten fresh on its own or squeezed for its juice. Certain varieties of orange can be turned into jam, and orange skin is used by the perfume and essence industries for its precious aromatic oils, as well as being candied for use in cakes and confectionery. Scented orange flower water is used in baking.

Of the many varieties, the best are Biondo Comune, Navel, Bella Donna and Valencia Late, which is much used in the jam and confectionery industry, although the bitter Seville orange is best. The main varieties of blood orange are the Tarocco, Sanguinello and Moro, which all have a deep-red pulp.

***Burro** / Butter*
Butter is obtained by collecting the cream off the top of the milk. After allowing the cream to undergo a little natural fermentation to develop flavour, it is put in a revolving container and churned until a clotted mass of the fat results, and the excess water discarded. This mass is then pressed into rectangular shapes for packaging.

Italian butter is generally unsalted and is especially flavoursome, particularly when made with Alpine milk. Butter is very much used in the making of cakes, biscuits and tarts, but is used in general cooking mainly in the North. Even there nowadays, however, it is suffering in competition with Southern olive oil for reasons of health. Butter is the dairy product with the highest fat content, at least 82%, and highly saturated.

***Candito** / Candied Fruit and Peel*
Candito is the name given to fruit or citrus rind that has been impregnated with a flavoured sugar syrup. In the lengthy and complicated procedure the sugar slowly replaces the water in the fruit, both preserving it and turning it into an edible sweet morsel. *Canditi* are used to make pastries in every Italian region. All sorts of fruit flans employ candied fruits of all types,

including cherries, strawberries, chestnuts, pears, apricots, whole clementines, and even certain varieties of pumpkin.

The most important candied peel, however, is that of the citrus fruits, like oranges, mandarins, lemons, and especially cedro or citron. Candied fruit, called *frutta candita*, is often served at the end of meals to be washed down with a little liqueur.

Castagna / Chestnut
In the past, chestnuts were used by the Italian peasant to enrich everyday meals such as soups, as well as being eaten as a vegetable or fruit. Because the chestnut has a rather neutral taste, it can be used in many ways, including being boiled and puréed for savoury stuffings, and with milk, sugar and whipped cream in the famous dessert, *montebianco*, which can be further enriched by the addition of Chantilly cream and alcohol. One of the classic recipes in which chestnuts are used is *caldallessa* or *ballotta*, a dish of freshly boiled chestnuts served with wine in Northern Italian trattorias or *enoteche* (wine bars) on 2 November. The nuts may also be simply boiled with a few bay leaves for 40-45 minutes, then peeled and eaten on their own.

Chestnuts can also be roasted (*caldarroste*), either in a pan over charcoal or in the oven. Whichever method you use, make sure you

make a small incision in the tough skin before cooking them to prevent the chestnuts from exploding. If you roast them in a pan, you will need a special roaster with holes in the bottom. Turn the chestnuts over the heat from time to time so that they roast evenly and do not burn, although if they develop a few black spots it will give them flavour. Charcoal-roasted chestnuts are often sold on street corners in the winter. If you cook them in the oven, they will get an overall browning and will be easier to peel. Do not cook them for too long, 30 minutes in a hot oven should be enough, or they will become hard and inedible.

Dried chestnuts need to be soaked for a day before being cooked in milk until soft, when they can either be eaten with salt as a savoury side dish or with vanilla, sugar and cinnamon as a dessert. Ground dried chestnuts can also be made into a flour which is used to make an unleavened cake, for the thickening of soups, and is sometimes mixed with wheat flour in the making of certain types of pasta. Chestnut flour is also mixed with water, sugar and vanilla to make *crema di castagne*, a filling for sweet ravioli.

Cedro / Citron
This citrus fruit looks like a large lemon and can weigh up to 1 kg (2 ¼ lb) and its rind can reach up to 3 cm (1¼ inches) in thickness. It is

grown in Calabria, Campania and Sicily for its peel, which is rich in aromatic oils and is mainly candied for use by the confectionery industry. See also page 35.

Ciliegia / Cherry
Cherries are mostly grown in Campania, Puglia, Emilia-Romagna and Veneto, all four regions exporting a huge number all over Europe. The main varieties grown are Durone Nero, Durone Nero di Vignola, Durone Nero di Anella and Amarena. Their need for particularly well-drained soil and hand-picking at harvest time makes them one of the most expensive fruits available. As well as being eaten on their own as a delicious fruit, cherries can also be preserved in pure alcohol or candied and coloured for use in confectionery. Cherries are also cooked with sugar and vanilla to make a dessert, as well as being used to make sauces for poultry and game.

Confettura, Marmellata / Jam, Marmalade
As in Britain, the Italians make a preserve similar to marmalade that uses oranges, lemons, tangerines, mandarins, clementines, grapefruits or limes. To earn the name *marmellata*, the preserve must only be made with the pulp, juice and rind of the fruit. By contrast, *confettura*, or jam, is made only with the pulp and juice of the fruit. The two are often confused, but to

add to the problem there is a third type of preserve called *gelatina*, a fruit jelly made with the strained juice of the fruit.

To make perfect jams and marmalades it is essential that the balance of sugar and the ripeness of the fruit are right, so it is important to use the ripest and the most perfect fruit you can find. If you add less sugar than the fruit needs, more water is extracted from the fruit in the cooking process, making it stronger in flavour but also more prone to fermentation and turning mouldy. My mother used to make a jam called *mostarda* (or *cugnà* in Piedmontese) from freshly pressed red grape juice and pears, prunes, peaches, quinces and even walnuts (see page 47). The fruit was mixed with sugar and vanilla and then cooked until it resembled a deep brown jam with a thick consistency. The taste was heavenly and we used to spread it liberally on buttered bread for *merenda*.

Cotogna, Cugna, Mela, Pera, Cotognata / *Quince, Quince Paste*

In the past, the quince was much used in the kitchen, especially to make sauces for roasted meats. Today, although it is still cultivated and is available on the market stalls of Italy in the autumn, it no longer holds the culinary position it once enjoyed. The small trees, with their regularly shaped leaves, bear pear- and apple-shaped fruit (hence the names *mela* or *pera*), with downy yellow skin that rubs down to a shine. It has a wonderful scent, although its flesh is too sour to eat raw and once cut it discolours rapidly, so a few drops of lemon juice need to be sprinkled over it.

It is possible to buy a commercially produced quince paste called *cotognata*, but it can be made at home by simply peeling the fruit, quartering it and cooking it in a little water with the zest of a lemon until the water has evaporated and the fruit is very soft. It may then be liquidized or mashed to a purée, mixed with the same quantity of sugar and reheated over a medium heat, stirring all the time to prevent it from sticking, until it turns a lovely reddish-brown. Spread the mixture on a flat surface and allow it to cool and dry for a couple of days, before cutting it into cubes and rolling it in coarsely crushed sugar. It can also be cooked with less sugar, orange juice and cinnamon to make a compote or jam. In Veneto they add mustard seeds and syrup to quince to make a preserve that is eaten with boiled chicken.

Fico / *Fig*

The finest figs are those eaten ripe from the plant, a rarity these days as so much fruit is picked unripe for long transportation – a particular issue with figs, which are extremely perishable. Originally from Syria, the fig was spread all over the world by the Romans and it is now grown in Italy in the regions of Puglia, Calabria and Sicily, where a few of the 700 available varieties are grown and eaten, either raw or preserved.

Figs can be either round or pear-shaped and some of them reach a considerable size, weighing up to 55-60 g (1¾ - 2 oz) each. The skin is very delicate and the inside of the fruit is made up of thousands of pods that produce a very sweet syrupy substance, giving the fruit its succulence. The best-known varieties grown in Italy are the Gentile Bianco, a Genovese variety which grows in Liguria, the Verdello, Brogiotto Bianco and Ottato. Fresh figs are very popular eaten simply as a fruit, with Parma ham (*prosciutto e fichi*) and in fruit salads and tarts.

Full of vitamins, the fig contains five times more calories by weight when dried than it does when fresh, and it is easier to transport and keep. Dried figs are obtained by drying the mature fruit in the sun, in an oven or in an air-drier, where all the water in the fruit is evaporated. Another way of preserving them is in a honey syrup, and these are exceptionally good eaten with a touch of cream as a dessert.

Fragola, Fragola Selvatica or di Bosco / *Strawberry, Wild Strawberry*

The strawberry grows outside, from spring through to autumn, but is now cultivated all year round in greenhouses. It perishes very quickly and should not be handled too much as it bruises easily. The best types of strawberry are the Gorella (a conical variety that is available from May), the rounder Pocahontas, the long and pointed Belruby and the Aliso, which grows mostly in the South, Emilia-Romagna, Piedmont, Veneto and Campania.

Wild strawberries, called *fragole di bosco*, grow in woodland areas. They are much smaller than the cultivated variety and have a much stronger flavour. They fetch a much higher price than commercially grown strawberries and, despite attempts to cultivate them, the real thing still cannot be beaten. Wild strawberries only need a little sugar and a few drops of lemon juice or balsamic vinegar as an accompaniment if they are eaten on their own, but they are also wonderful in fruit tarts and in all the same recipes using cultivated strawberry, such as confectionery, liqueurs, preserves, jams and gelatines. Strawberries may also be candied and used as a filling and decoration for many cakes, sweets and desserts.

Gelato / Ice-Cream

The practice of preserving snow in caves was brought to Sicily by the Arabs. There also snow was mixed with citrus fruit pulp to make early sorbets. The Romans then developed the techniques of mixing snow and ice with fruit and honey.

In 1533, Caterina de Medici took this, among many other culinary novelties, with her to France when she married Henri II.

It was, however, a Sicilian, Francesco Procopio, who opened a café in Paris at which new techniques were used to produce real ice-cream, based on cream, eggs and sugar, as we know it today. However, the invention of this product has actually been credited to a French chef of the British King Charles 1, in 1650.

Today ice-cream is synonymous with Italy, where the best artisanal ice-cream is produced. The most famous *gelaterie* are still to be found in Campania and Sicily. Also, like *pizzerie*, you can find Italian-run ice-cream parlours all over the world.

Lampone / Raspberry

The fruit of a bushy plant that grows in the hills of Italy at an altitude of up to 1,500 metres (4,500 feet), the raspberry needs a cool climate to grow well. Like strawberries, they are perishable and delicate, and should be handled as little as possible. They are made up of a collection of tiny pods, each of which contains a seed. The berry is attached to a conical white stem from which it can only be pulled cleanly when the fruit is quite ripe.

The flavour of the raspberry is so intense that it is mostly used to make syrups and jellies for the confectionery industry, but they are also delicious raw on tarts, on

meringues, in fruit salad or, best of all, on their own. If cooked with sugar they make a wonderful sauce for ice-cream or creamy desserts, as well as making wonderful sorbets themselves. Agricultural and technological advancements have made commercial cultivation of this fruit easier and much of the new abundant crop is frozen to make sauces, syrups and gelatines.

Lima, Limetta / Lime

This citrus fruit has only recently gained access to Italy, especially in Sicily where they are being grown experimentally. Smaller than a lemon, the lime has a smoother dark green colour and a highly scented rind which is used to savour drinks, as well as sauces for fish. The juice is less pungent than that of the lemon and is used in delicate dishes, again especially with fish. Very recently, also, a liqueur has been produced using the very intensely perfumed oils extracted from the skin.

Limone / Lemon

Originally from Asia, the lemon found its way to Europe via the Middle East and was probably introduced by the Arabs. Sicily produces 90 per cent of Italy's lemons (650,000 tonnes per year), and the other 10 per cent are grown in Calabria and Sardinia, with some of the best coming from the Amalfi coast in Campania. Lemon varieties have quite funny names, like

Femminello, Femminello di Santa Teresa, Monachello and Interdonato.

Lemons are well known for being rich in vitamin C and they are so acidic that their juice can corrode iron and be used as a disinfectant. In the kitchen, however, it is the ability of the lemon to flavour and to sour, as well as to prevent oxidation, that is most valued. Lemon juice is used to heighten the flavour of both sweet and savoury sauces.

The aroma and flavour of the lemon is at its strongest in the skin. The drinks, confectionery and bakery industries make good use of the oils extracted from the skin in juices, jams and extracts. I often use lemon rind infused in hot water to make canarino, which is a wonderful tonic.

Mandarino, Mandarancio, Clementina, Mandarinetto / Mandarin, Satsuma, Clementine

The mandarin has been joined by two very similar fruits, the satsuma and the clementine, but neither can match the flavour and juiciness of the seedless flesh of the thin-skinned original. This popular citrus fruit comes from China and is now cultivated with great success in Calabria and Sicily, which together produce 75 per cent of the national yield. The rest is grown in Campania, Basilicata, Puglia and Sardinia, although it is now being replaced, at least in part, by the new hybrids.

The clementine is smaller and satsuma larger than the mandarin,

and both have a wonderful, deep-orange skin and are rounder than the mandarin. The best-known varieties of mandarin are the Avena, Tardivo di Ciaculli, Tardivo della Conca d'Oro, while the best-known clementine varieties are Comuni, Clementine Monreales, Clementine di Nules and Clementine Orovales. The satsuma – a seedless version of the tangerine with more compact pulp – is used in the same way as the mandarin. Its culture is fairly recent in Italy.

The technique used in the culture of mandarins of continually watering the plants on a drip system means that the fruit can be adequately irrigated. The fruit is harvested between November and January, for consumption about a month later, especially at Christmas. A variety of commercial operations have grown up around the cultivation of mandarins, including the making of juices, aromatic oils, pulp and candied peel, all for use in the drinks, confectionery and cosmetic industries.

The smallest variety of mandarin, called mandarinetto, used to be candied whole, resulting in a delicious confection with a slightly resilient skin and a very sugary centre.

Mandorla / Almond

Common all around the Mediterranean and in Asia, the almond was introduced into Italy by the ancient Greeks, along with the vine and the fig tree. The

almond tree has many similarities with the peach tree, with leaves of the same shape and the same type of wood. When it is growing and forming, the nut is contained within a pointed oval stone that is encased within a thick green outer skin, called mallo.

Due to its combination of proteins, minerals and high fat content (50 per cent), the almond has been a valuable food for thousands of years. A number of varieties, including Tuono, Filippo Ceo and Ferrangnes, are cultivated in Sicily, Veneto, Puglia, Campania and Sardinia.

There are two types of almond: the sweet and the bitter. The bitter almond is the smaller of the two and has the typical almond taste, which is used to boost the flavour of all products made with sweet almonds. It has to be heat-treated before use, however, as otherwise it is toxic.

Among the best-known almond products is marzipan (pasta reale or pasta di mandorle, see opposite and page 28), which is much used in the south. The almond is particularly favoured in Sicily, where it is used to make the famous Cassata (see page 38), as well as biscuits and torrone.

The very precious oil from almonds is used both in pâtisserie to flavour sweets and in medicines and cosmetics for its softening properties. There is also a kind of milk that is extracted from the almond which is used to make a drink called latte di mandorle. It resembles coconut milk and is extremely delicious.

Almonds are also used in the making of Amaretto, a famous liqueur, and Amaretti biscuits. Both of these products require a large number of bitter almonds and fewer of the balancing sweetness of the other variety.

Marzapane, Pasta Reale / Marzipan

This paste of sugar, almond flour and egg white is widely used in Sicily to make *cassata siciliana* and to bake a variety of biscuits. It is also used as filling for tarts and dates. Marzipan has a sweetish taste, only sometimes betraying a hint of the bitter almonds or *armelline* added to enhance the almond flavour. In certain parts of the South, marzipan is called *pasta reale* ('royal paste'), indicating the regard with which it was held. A Sicilian variation called *frutta di marturana* is based on marzipan shaped into all types of fruit which are then given the original colours.

Mascarpone, Mascherpone / Cream Cheese

Initially only made in southern Lombardy, in the province of Lodi, mascarpone is now produced in various Italian regions. Made within 24 hours from pasteurized cream coagulated with citric or 5 per cent tartaric acid, it is a very soft cheese which once it is made has to be consumed immediately. One hundred litres (22 gallons) of cream produce 40-50 kg (90-110 lb) of mascarpone with a fat content of 50 per cent and above.

Mascarpone is seldom used as cheese, but is extremely valuable as an ingredient for sweets and desserts, one of the most famous being tiramisu. In the past it was packed in small fabric containers, but it is now sold in jars or plastic containers.

Mela / Apple

By far the most frequently eaten fruit in Italy – probably in Europe – is the apple. Of the total weight of 100 kg (220 lb) of fruit eaten by each Italian every year, at least half is apples. There are over 250 varieties of apple, a fruit that is considered to be one of the healthiest, with its high level of fibre, vitamin C and acidity.

Fifty per cent of Italian apples are cultivated in the Trentino Alto Adige, with Emilia-Romagna, Veneto, Piedmont, Lombardy and Campania contributing the remaining half. Apple trees need cool temperatures and little wind, which is why they are cultivated in tranquil valleys and the flatlands of the north. The varieties grown in Italy meet local requirements, so they may be different to those grown in other parts of the world.

The first harvest in July includes varieties like Gravenstein, Ozark Gold and the succulent Golden Red apple. These are followed in autumn by Golden Delicious, Red Delicious, the very red Stayman, the extremely green Granny Smith and the huge Imperatore. My favourite apple is the Reneste/Reveste, a rusty yellow apple with a yellowish pulp and a very developed flavour, which stays juicy and firm all winter. Most apples keep for quite a long time, up to a month if stored in a well-ventilated, temperature-controlled room.

As well as being eaten on its own, the apple is much used in the making of sauces, compotes, pies, tarts and other baking, as well as in juices and in the manufacture of brandy.

Mirtillo / Blueberry

Pollution has made this berry difficult to find growing in the wild and there is little interest in hunting out the few that are left, which means that the only blueberries you can get are the larger commercially cultivated ones. These are available all year round but they lack the flavour of the real thing. In the wild, the blueberry grows through the summer into the autumn in the hills and mountains over 1,500 metres (4,500 ft) high. The blue-black berries are very small and a special wooden comb is used to collect them in order to avoid damaging the structure of the plant.

The cultivated blueberry from America is much bigger, with a more distinct bluish tinge to the skin and paler flesh. They can be eaten on their own or with other wild berries in the fruit salad known as *sottobosco*, or to fill fruit tarts. They are also used to make a sauce for game and poultry, a jam called *confettura di mirtilli*, a sweet sauce for pâtisserie and, finally, a liqueur.

Mora di Rovo / Blackberry
In summer, it is common to see Italians making their way through thorny brambles to collect wild blackberries. Agricultural progress means that it is now possible to buy cultivated blackberries, grown on thornless bushes for much easier picking.

Although it is less flavoursome than the wild variety, the cultivated blackberry is still good in fruit salads and as a topping for fruit tarts, as well as making delicious jams, compotes, juices and syrups for use in the liqueur, pâtisserie and confectionery industries.

Nocciola, Avellana / Hazelnut
The city of Avellino in Campania takes its name from the product for which it is celebrated, the hazelnut. The hazelnut tree comes from Turkey, but has been successfully adapted to grow in various part of Italy. More than half of the 100,000 tonnes produced each year come from Campania. The rest comes from Lazio, Piedmont and Sicily, where the nuts are particularly good. The variety called Tonda Gentile delle Langhe grows in the same area as the white truffle and it is said that the truffles which

grow beside hazelnut trees are the best. Other varieties include Mortarelle, Gentile Romana and Nostrale di Sicilia.

Hazelnuts ripen in autumn. The round kernel is encased in a tough wooden husk so it keeps for a long time although, like all foods that contain fat, it will turn rancid and go bad if it is badly kept. The nuts are very nutritious, containing a balance of fat (600 calories per 100 g/3½ oz), protein, vitamins and minerals. In Piedmont, the best hazelnuts are roasted then ground into an extremely fine paste to make nougat and Gianduiotti chocolate. They are also used in a huge number of biscuits and cakes all over the country.

Noce / Walnut
The best Italian walnuts come from the Sorrento area in Campania and the best variety is the eponymous Sorrento, a large nut with a thin, easily breakable shell and very tasty nut. Other good varieties include the late-ripening Sorrento Giovanni and a French variety called Franquette.

The nut grows in bunches from large trees that came originally from Asia and are as much sought after for their wood as their fruit. The nut is formed inside a fleshy green outer skin called *mallo* which peels open when the nut is ripe, around September or October, allowing the nut, protected by its hard, wrinkled casing, to fall to the

ground. Inside, the nut is divided into four sections, called *gherigli*.

Fresh walnuts are delicious, as long as you remove the nut from the bitter yellow skin surrounding it. To enjoy the full flavour of the walnut, however, it is better to wait until it is completely dry, when the nut will have shrunk inside the shell and the yellow skin turned brown and papery. The best nuts are those of the last crop before the oils in the nut turn rancid.

Walnuts are used to make biscuits, cakes and confectionery. They are also served at Christmastime with dried fruits such as dates, hazelnuts and apricots. Finally, the oil extracted from the walnut is used to make tasty salad dressings.

Pasta Reale, see Marzapane

Pera / Pear
The pear originated from the area around the Caspian Sea and was introduced into Europe about 2,000 years ago. Today there are around 5,000 varieties, and Italy is one of the biggest of the world's producers, cultivating about ten varieties. Nearly two-thirds of all the pears cultivated in Italy come from Emilia-Romagna, with Campania, Veneto, Lazio, Sicily, Lombardy and Piedmont making up the balance.

Early varieties, maturing around July, include Coscia, Butirra Morettini and Guyot, all of which have a juicy flesh and yellow skin.In August the red or yellow Williams pear ripens and is followed by the winter varieties such as the Abate, the orangey-yellow Kaiser and the large Decana del Comizio or Comice, and finally the largest and longest-keeping, green-yellow pear, Passa Crassana. While these are all grown commercially, the small and delicious rusty-coloured St Martin from Piedmont is worth looking out for. Winter varieties can be kept for a few months if properly stored, but summer fruit should be eaten when ripe.

Pesca, Pescanoce / *Peach, Nectarine*

The Mediterranean region, and Italy in particular, seems to be ideal for growing peaches and their cousins the nectarines. The tree was originally brought to the area from Persia by Alexander the Great, but now Italy produces about 80 per cent of Europe's total consumption, despite being avid consumers of the fruit themselves. There are two major types of peach, although there are many varieties. The first type is Pesca Comune di Pasta Bianca, the common peach, an apple-sized fruit with a thin downy skin and a white, juicy and deliciously scented flesh. The second variety is much like the first but has a yellow flesh and a reddish-yellow skin.

Other types of peach include the Percoca, a peach from the south with a yellowy-green skin and a firm flesh that is widely used by the preserving industry, and the wild Pesche di Vigna that grows alone in the vineyards of Italy. The latter has a very intense flavour and is usually white-fleshed with a green-and-red skin. This lovely peach can be prised into two halves and popped straight into your mouth because it is so small. Vineyard owners try to keep these peach trees, with their beautifully scented pink flowers, hidden away so that they can enjoy their fruit fresh or preserved in syrup for Christmas.

The nectarine is not a hybrid, but a true variety of peach. It is very similar but has a completely smooth and shiny skin. Again, there are two main types, one with white and the other with yellow flesh, and countless varieties have been developed to crop from May to September. In the end, however, the peach has much more flavour.

Pistacchio / *Pistachio Nut*

The pistachio is the fruit of a wonderful little tree that is typical of the southern Mediterranean and unique in Italy to the island of Sicily, the only region with the right climatic conditions for its growth. The nuts grows in bundles enclosed within a fleshy red pod that bursts open to reveal the nut bulging out of its woody envelope. Inside, the pistachio is actually bright green, which makes it ideal for decorating cakes, biscuits and other sweets. It is also used as a stuffing for meat, and even finds its way into the salami, Mortadella. The nut is also ground into a powder and used as the base for a very tasty ice-cream and, to prove its versatility, it is also popular eaten salted as a snack with drinks.

Prugna, Susina, Prugna Secca / *Plums, Prunes*

In Italian, the words *prugna* and *susina* are both used to refer to plums, while *prugna secca* is the name given to prunes. The plum originates from Asia but grows very successfully all over Europe, as well as many other parts of the world. Italy produces about 150,000 tonnes a year, concentrating on Regina Claudia (greengages, my preference, with their sweet flesh and green skin), Prugna d'Italia, Precoce die Guignao, Formosa, Dane Aubert, Santarosa Stanley, Blue Gestetter and California Blue. The main regions for plum cultivation are Emilia-Romagna, Campania, Morele, Alto Adige and Piedmont.

Ribes / *Blackcurrants, Redcurrants, White Currants*

These soft summer fruits come from a bushy plant that can be found in the wild. The translucent black, red or white berries are collected in small bunches. The blackcurrant is used by the drinks industry to make an alcoholic syrup that can be diluted with wine or spumante to make kir or for making jams. In jam-making, because of their high pectin content, *ribes* are often added to low-pectin fruit like strawberries and peaches. They are used in pâtisserie, in fruit tarts, and for decorating sweets. Along with other berry fruit, they are used in summery fruit salads.

Ricotta / *Soft Cheese*
As is suggested by its name, meaning literally 'cooked again', this cheese is the product of other cheeses using the residue left after the curd has been lifted. Fresh milk is added to this residue to give a higher yield and then the mixture is brought to the boil. An acidic agent like lemon juice or rennet is then added, and when casein froth forms on the surface it is scooped off and allowed to drain. This froth is the cheese.

Uva, Uva da Tavola, Uvetta, Sultanina / *Grape, Raisin, Sultana*
There is an unbelievable variety of grapes grown in the world; some are cultivated exclusively for wine making, while others are for eating as a fruit – *uva da tavola* or table grapes. While it is possible to eat wine grapes at the table, table grapes cannot be used to make wine, however. The Romans took this vital plant with them everywhere they went, introducing it to France and many other countries as they conquered Europe. Italy is now the biggest producer of grapes in the world,

followed by Spain and France. The best-known and most successful table grape is the Italia, which – thanks to new techniques for delaying ripening – is available from August to December. It is much appreciated in Italy and Europe, where it is exported in large quantities to Germany and France. Other varieties include the Uva Regina, the Red Cardinal, Primus and Baresana.

More than half of the grapes grown in Italy come from the fertile region of Puglia, with Sicily, Abruzzi, Lazio, Basilicata, Calabria and Sardinia making up the difference. Together they produce 1,400,000 tonnes of grapes a year, of which 450,000 are exported. In Piedmont, Veneto and most of the other wine-grape-producing regions, wonderfully ripe grapes like Uva Americana, Fragola (with the scent of strawberries) and the very sweet Moscato are often sold locally. I think the only variety worth eating is the Muscat. Bunches are hung on strong string until they turn from golden yellow to a wrinkled golden brown, when they become intensely and deliciously sweet. In Italy it is widely considered to be good luck to eat grapes on New Year's Eve and, although I am not really superstitious, I still do it now (sadly, however, not with the same quality of grapes).

More and more foreign varieties are taking over, including the

popular seedless Thompson variety. Today, the vast quantity of winter grapes sold lack flavour. Table grapes are eaten raw as dessert, or in fruit salads, or to cover fruit tarts. Some of the grapes are preserved in alcohol and served in a little bowl with a little of the liquor.

When they are dried, grapes turn into *uvetta* or raisins and sultanina or sultanas, which are often made with seedless grapes. The largest sultana is the pale-blonde Malaga, which has a few seeds, and the smallest raisin is the seedless blue-black Corinth, which is imported from the Middle East. Both raisins and sultanas are used in pâtisserie, featuring in a range of recipes, including *panettone*, as well as being used with ricotta in sweet fillings for tarts and cakes. They also make a delicious snack when soaked in brandy or rum.

Probably the most sought-after raisin to eat by itself is that made from the Zibibbo grape, the fruit of a vine grown in Italy for the making of the famous Moscato di Pantelleria. The raisins are dried still attached to the stalks.

Uva Spina / *Gooseberry*
This spiky bush is related to the redcurrant. The berries are delicious when golden-yellow and ripe, but are only grown privately in Italy. They can be eaten in pies, cooked with sugar as a dessert, and used to make gooseberry fool.

Index

Publishing Director: Anne Furniss
Creative Director: Mary Evans
Editor: Lewis Esson
Consultant Art Director: Helen Lewis
Design: Sue Storey
Cover Design: Claire Peters
Assistant Editor: Jane Middleton
Editorial Assistant: Rhian Bromage
Production: Sarah Neesam &
                Vincent Smith

This edition first published in 2013 by
Quadrille Publishing Limited,
Alhambra House,
27-31 Charing Cross Road,
London WC2H OLS

Based on material originally published
in *Carluccio's Complete Italian Food.*

Text © 1997 & 1999 Carluccio's
Partnership
Photography © 1997 Estate of
André Martin
Cover Illustrations © 2013
Zack Blanton
Design, edited text and layout © 1999,
2013 Quadrille Publishing Ltd

Cataloguing-in-Publication Data: a
catalogue record for this book is
available from the British Library.

ISBN 978 184949 483 0

Printed in China.